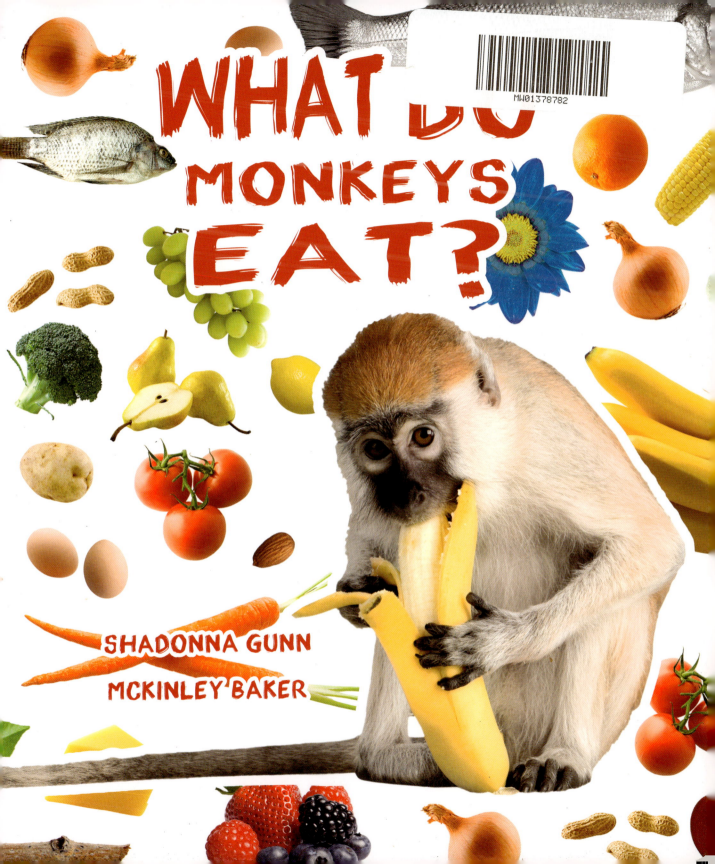

# WHAT DO MONKEYS EAT?

SHADONNA GUNN
MCKINLEY BAKER

Barbary macaque

root

Some monkeys eat roots.

**Proboscis monkey**

vegetables

Some monkeys eat vegetables.

3

Gelada baboon

bugs

Some monkeys eat bugs.

Howler monkey

fruit

Some monkeys eat fruit.

5

Red Colobus monkey

leaves

Some monkeys eat leaves.

Some monkeys eat nuts.

**Squirrel monkey**

seeds

Some monkeys eat seeds.

berries

Some monkeys eat berries.

# Crab-eating macaque

flower

Some monkeys eat flowers.

Langur monkey

bark

Some monkeys eat bark.

**Vervet monkey**

egg

Some monkeys eat eggs.

Lion-tailed macaque

lizard

Some monkeys eat lizards.

Hamadryas baboon

fish

Some monkeys eat fish.

Olive baboon

poop

Some monkeys eat poop!

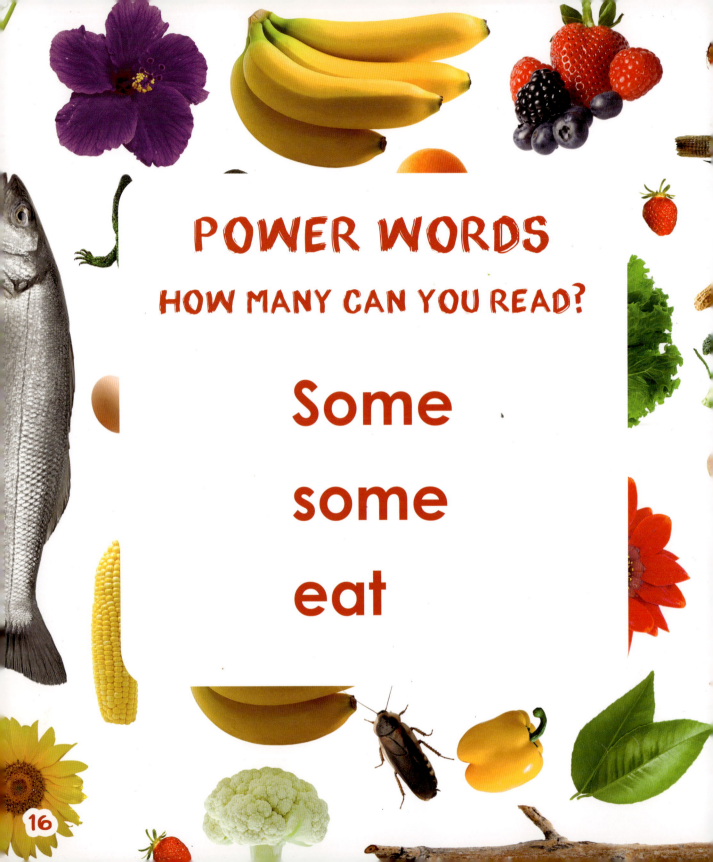

# POWER WORDS
## HOW MANY CAN YOU READ?

# Some
# some
# eat